HowExpert

How To Homeschool

Your Step By Step Guide To Homeschooling

HowExpert with Jane Rodda

Copyright HowExpert™
www.HowExpert.com

For more tips related to this topic, visit HowExpert.com/homeschool.

Recommended Resources

- HowExpert.com – Quick 'How To' Guides on All Topics from A to Z by Everyday Experts.
- HowExpert.com/free – Free HowExpert Email Newsletter.
- HowExpert.com/books – HowExpert Books
- HowExpert.com/courses – HowExpert Courses
- HowExpert.com/clothing – HowExpert Clothing
- HowExpert.com/membership – HowExpert Membership Site
- HowExpert.com/affiliates – HowExpert Affiliate Program
- HowExpert.com/writers – Write About Your #1 Passion/Knowledge/Expertise & Become a HowExpert Author.
- HowExpert.com/resources – Additional HowExpert Recommended Resources
- YouTube.com/HowExpert – Subscribe to HowExpert YouTube.
- Instagram.com/HowExpert – Follow HowExpert on Instagram.
- Facebook.com/HowExpert – Follow HowExpert on Facebook.

From the Publisher

Dear HowExpert reader,

HowExpert publishes quick 'how to' guides on all topics from A to Z by everyday experts.

At HowExpert, our mission is to discover, empower, and maximize talents of everyday people to ultimately make a positive impact in the world for all topics from A to Z...one everyday expert at a time!

All of our HowExpert guides are written by everyday people just like you and me who have a passion, knowledge, and expertise for a specific topic.

We take great pride in selecting everyday experts who have a passion, great writing skills, and knowledge about a topic that they love to be able to teach you about the topic you are also passionate about and eager to learn about.

We hope you get a lot of value from our HowExpert guides and it can make a positive impact in your life in some kind of way. All of our readers including you altogether help us continue living our mission of making a positive impact in the world for all spheres of influences from A to Z.

If you enjoyed one of our HowExpert guides, then please take a moment to send us your feedback from wherever you got this book.

Thank you and we wish you all the best in all aspects of life.

Sincerely,

BJ Min
Founder & Publisher of HowExpert
HowExpert.com

PS...If you are also interested in becoming a HowExpert author, then please visit our website at HowExpert.com/writers. Thank you & again, all the best!

COPYRIGHT, LEGAL NOTICE AND DISCLAIMER:

COPYRIGHT © BY HOWEXPERT™ (OWNED BY HOT METHODS). ALL RIGHTS RESERVED WORLDWIDE. NO PART OF THIS PUBLICATION MAY BE REPRODUCED IN ANY FORM OR BY ANY MEANS, INCLUDING SCANNING, PHOTOCOPYING, OR OTHERWISE WITHOUT PRIOR WRITTEN PERMISSION OF THE COPYRIGHT HOLDER.

DISCLAIMER AND TERMS OF USE: PLEASE NOTE THAT MUCH OF THIS PUBLICATION IS BASED ON PERSONAL EXPERIENCE AND ANECDOTAL EVIDENCE. ALTHOUGH THE AUTHOR AND PUBLISHER HAVE MADE EVERY REASONABLE ATTEMPT TO ACHIEVE COMPLETE ACCURACY OF THE CONTENT IN THIS GUIDE, THEY ASSUME NO RESPONSIBILITY FOR ERRORS OR OMISSIONS. ALSO, YOU SHOULD USE THIS INFORMATION AS YOU SEE FIT, AND AT YOUR OWN RISK. YOUR PARTICULAR SITUATION MAY NOT BE EXACTLY SUITED TO THE EXAMPLES ILLUSTRATED HERE; IN FACT, IT'S LIKELY THAT THEY WON'T BE THE SAME, AND YOU SHOULD ADJUST YOUR USE OF THE INFORMATION AND RECOMMENDATIONS ACCORDINGLY.

THE AUTHOR AND PUBLISHER DO NOT WARRANT THE PERFORMANCE, EFFECTIVENESS OR APPLICABILITY OF ANY SITES LISTED OR LINKED TO IN THIS BOOK. ALL LINKS ARE FOR INFORMATION PURPOSES ONLY AND ARE NOT WARRANTED FOR CONTENT, ACCURACY OR ANY OTHER IMPLIED OR EXPLICIT PURPOSE.

ANY TRADEMARKS, SERVICE MARKS, PRODUCT NAMES OR NAMED FEATURES ARE ASSUMED TO BE THE PROPERTY OF THEIR RESPECTIVE OWNERS, AND ARE USED ONLY FOR REFERENCE. THERE IS NO IMPLIED ENDORSEMENT IF WE USE ONE OF THESE TERMS.

NO PART OF THIS BOOK MAY BE REPRODUCED, STORED IN A RETRIEVAL SYSTEM, OR TRANSMITTED BY ANY OTHER MEANS: ELECTRONIC, MECHANICAL, PHOTOCOPYING, RECORDING, OR OTHERWISE, WITHOUT THE PRIOR WRITTEN PERMISSION OF THE AUTHOR.

ANY VIOLATION BY STEALING THIS BOOK OR DOWNLOADING OR SHARING IT ILLEGALLY WILL BE PROSECUTED BY LAWYERS TO THE FULLEST EXTENT. THIS PUBLICATION IS PROTECTED UNDER THE US COPYRIGHT ACT OF 1976 AND ALL OTHER APPLICABLE INTERNATIONAL, FEDERAL, STATE AND LOCAL LAWS AND ALL RIGHTS ARE RESERVED, INCLUDING RESALE RIGHTS: YOU ARE NOT ALLOWED TO GIVE OR SELL THIS GUIDE TO ANYONE ELSE.

THIS PUBLICATION IS DESIGNED TO PROVIDE ACCURATE AND AUTHORITATIVE INFORMATION WITH REGARD TO THE SUBJECT MATTER COVERED. IT IS SOLD WITH THE UNDERSTANDING THAT THE AUTHORS AND PUBLISHERS ARE NOT ENGAGED IN RENDERING LEGAL, FINANCIAL, OR OTHER PROFESSIONAL ADVICE. LAWS AND PRACTICES OFTEN VARY FROM STATE TO STATE AND IF LEGAL OR OTHER EXPERT ASSISTANCE IS REQUIRED, THE SERVICES OF A PROFESSIONAL SHOULD BE SOUGHT. THE AUTHORS AND PUBLISHER SPECIFICALLY DISCLAIM ANY LIABILITY THAT IS INCURRED FROM THE USE OR APPLICATION OF THE CONTENTS OF THIS BOOK.

COPYRIGHT BY HOWEXPERT™ (OWNED BY HOT METHODS)
ALL RIGHTS RESERVED WORLDWIDE.

Table of Contents

Recommended Resources 2
From the Publisher 3
Introduction 7
   What is Homeschooling? 7
   Upside to Homeschooling 7
   Downside to Homeschooling 8
   How the Guide is Arranged 9
      A Look In 9
      Step-By-Step Guide 10
      What to Do 10
      What Not To Do 10
Chapter 1: Making The Decision 12
   A Look In On Making the Decision 12
      Step-By-Step Guide to Making the Decision 14
      What to Do 15
      What Not To Do 16
Chapter 2: Getting Started 17
   A Look In On Getting Started 17
      Step-By-Step Guide to Getting Started 18
      What to Do 18
      What Not To Do 19
Chapter 3: Choosing Your Curriculum 20
   A Look In On Choosing Your Curriculum 20
      Step-By-Step Guide to Choosing Your
      Curriculum 21
      What to Do 22
      What Not To Do 23
Chapter 4: Schedules 24

    A Look In On Schedules 24
        Step-By-Step Guide to Schedules 26
        What to Do 27
        What Not To Do 27
Chapter 5: Assessment 29
    A Look In On Assessment 29
        Step-By-Step Guide to Assessment 31
        What to Do 31
        What Not To Do 32
Chapter 6: Socializing 33
    A Look In On Socializing 33
        Step-By-Step Guide to Socializing 35
        What to Do 36
        What Not To Do 36
Chapter 7: Legal Issues 38
    A Look In On Legal Issues 38
        Step-By-Step Guide to Legal Issues 39
        What to Do 39
        What Not To Do 40
Conclusion 41
    A Look In On Homeschooling 41
        Top 9 Things to Remember 42
About the Expert 48
Recommended Resources 49

Introduction

What is Homeschooling?

Education is a staple of every culture. Whether the teaching is done in a school, at home, by the village, or any combination of the three, children are educated. They are educated in the values and traditions and resources that are necessary for each culture to survive. The concept of education is traced back far into history, with early Greek civilization placing a great emphasis on the need to educate children. Aristotle is quoted as saying, "Those who educate children are to be honored more than those who produce them. For one only gave them life, the other, the art of living well."

The ways of educating children are varied, with options ranging from homeschooling to traditional public school to private schools to boarding schools, and everything in between.

Many parents these days take the approach of homeschooling their children. Homeschooling is exactly what it sounds like – children are schooled in the home.

Upside to Homeschooling

Although at times the idea of homeschooling has been controversial, I believe that there are many upsides to it. The main benefit is that you, the parent, have control over what your children are learning. You know their strengths and weaknesses, their passions and interests, and what method works best with them. You can tailor the schooling to each child's need, and your children do not run the risk of being lost in the crowd of a classroom.

Another upside of homeschooling is that you get to have more time together as a family. My husband and I are very involved with youth work, and the majority of our work is done during the hours that school is not in session. If my children were in traditional school, we would have to choose between spending time with the youth we serve or our own family. Our choice to homeschool has allowed us to have more time with our children.

The final upside that I will mention is that by homeschooling, you get to have the pleasure of watching your children learn. There is something so exciting about the moment when you see your child's face light up, and hear the words, "OH! I get it!" As a former teacher, I have encountered this with many children, but there is nothing as sweet as seeing it in my own kids. I would be sad to miss out on these opportunities.

Downside to Homeschooling

The main downside to homeschooling is that it takes a lot of work, commitment, and dedication on the part of the parents to ensure that the children are learning and growing. It is not easy coming up with different lesson plans and curriculum for each of my children. Some days it is not easy keeping my children motivated to learn. We do have days when I think it would be a whole lot easier to send them to a traditional school.

Another downside to homeschooling is that it is easy to feel isolated. I have to make an effort to leave the house and make sure that my children have regular interaction with their peers. It would be easy to just remain inside our family bubble, but I know that this is not what is best for my family. I also know that after a week without interacting with the outside world, I feel like I am losing my mind, and getting out is a necessity!

How the Guide is Arranged

I have arranged this guide into different chapters, with each chapter addressing a different issue that comes along with homeschooling. Each chapter is then divided into four different sections. I will explain what each section entails.

A Look In

This section gives a look into my life and experience as a homeschooler. I have been homeschooling my own children for five years, and have also been asked at times to homeschool other children (which I suppose would be more aptly named

Neighborschool, but that's not the main issue). In these sections I share my own story to help you learn from my mistakes and accomplishments.

Step-By-Step Guide

This section is exactly what it sounds like. It is a short, actionable list which will help you get started, make changes to your current routine, or encourage you so that you know you are not alone in what you are doing.

What to Do

This section includes specific ideas and actions of what you should do to make your homeschooling journey a success.

What Not To Do

This section, as I'm sure is obvious, gives specific things that you should avoid doing. These tips are given straight from my own experience. Hopefully you can avoid the mistakes that I have made!

I hope you enjoy reading this guide, and that it will help you will find as much joy and excitement in homeschooling as I have.

Chapter 1: Making The Decision

A Look In On Making the Decision

I will never forget the night that I made the decision to homeschool my children. My oldest, who is now nine years old, was three. He was playing in the living room, and my husband and I were watching something on television. Suddenly I burst into tears.

My husband, quite appropriately, looked at me like I was absolutely crazy. We were not watching a sad show, and there was really no reason for me to be crying. I wasn't pregnant, and our youngest at the time was nine months old and I was past the post partum period, so all of the reasons that had caused me to cry unexpectedly and uncontrollably in the past were no longer viable.

After recovering from his shock, he asked me what had me so upset, and I told him that I was sad because our son was going to go to school. Now, much to my husband's credit, he didn't laugh at me when he pointed out that we were still two years away from our son starting kindergarten. He heard my concern, and we started the discussion as to why I was so upset.

My husband asked me some questions to help me discover what bothered me so much. Was I sad that my son would grow up? Was I worried that he'd be hurt? Or was it something else?

After much discussion, I was able to inform my husband that I was jealous that other teachers would be able to have the joy of watching our son learn. I told him that I loved being a teacher but also loved being home with our children, and I longed to have the joy of educating our children like I had educated children in the classroom. I said that I realized that there were qualified teachers out there, but that I was also a qualified teacher and wondered why we'd give up time with our children to have other adults do what I was perfectly capable of doing.

And then he asked the question that started it all. "Why don't we homeschool?" The minute he asked it I knew it was right for our family. Up until that point, I had never really thought about homeschooling as being a realistic option for our family. Both my husband and I had worked as classroom teachers, and my husband was working as a substitute teacher, and I had just assumed that public school was what we would do. But the minute my husband suggested it, I knew it was what we would do.

I jumped into the homeschooling idea with both feet. I bought books, researched online, and created my plan of action for my family. I discovered what I liked about the idea of homeschooling, and what I didn't like about the idea of homeschooling. I took the time to talk with other homeschooling parents and with public school teachers, and I made note of areas that I should pay attention to.

Once I made the decision, I stuck with it. I realized that I could change my mind later if I wanted to, but that if I was going to homeschool I was going to do it with my full effort and attention. I've never once looked back.

Step-By-Step Guide to Making the Decision

1. Determine why you are considering homeschooling.

    Are you looking to homeschool because you want more time with family? Are you afraid of the change that will come when your children start school? Are you unhappy with the public school system? Are you surrounded by homeschoolers and feel bad sending your child to public school? Consider the reasons that you are homeschooling to make sure that everyone will benefit from your decision, and that it is done in the best interest of your family, and not for anyone else.

2. Assess your relationship with your children.

    Do you have the ability to be firm and enforce the importance of education? Do you enjoy being at home with your children? Will you be fulfilled by being a full time teacher?

3. Assess your abilities.

    Do you feel confident in your ability to educate your children? Do you have experience in a teaching capacity? Do you value education and learning? Do you have the patience to help your child struggle through lessons?

4. Discuss the decision with your spouse.

   Does your spouse agree with your decision to homeschool? Will your spouse support you in your endeavor? Is your spouse prepared to help enforce the idea that education is important and that there is a time to sit down and focus on learning?

5. Discuss the decision with your children.

   I firmly believe that parents know what is best for their children, and that parents should have the final say in decisions made for their family. However, this decision should be discussed with your children. Are they okay with the idea? Will they enjoy having more time at home? Are they willing to sacrifice being around their peers? What are they afraid of with homeschooling? What are they excited about?

What to Do

Making the decision to homeschool was very easy for me. It may be easy for you as well, or it may be more difficult. Her are just a few things to remember:

- Realize that discussing the option doesn't lock you into anything.
- Be honest with yourself in regards to your strengths and weaknesses.
- Make sure that the choice you are making will benefit your child.
- Keep the discussion open.
- Follow your gut.

What Not To Do

- Do not make the decision because you are feeling pressured to do so.
- Do not let others who are not a part of your core family make the decision for you. Input is fine, but they do not live your life, and they do not know what is best for you.
- Do not worry what others will think. A large portion of my extended family has not supported my decision to homeschool. I have heard every insult imaginable, but I know that the decision is best for my family, and my children are thriving.
- Do not close your mind to other schooling options. If there comes a time when another teacher can offer more to my children, I will step aside.
- Do not feel that your decision is permanent. If you try homeschooling and it doesn't work for your family, then change the schooling arrangement.

Chapter 2: Getting Started

A Look In On Getting Started

Once I made the decision to homeschool, I jumped into reading as many books as I could. I found online forums for homeschooling families, talked with my friends who were homeschooling, and looked at the options that I had available to me.

I also started setting the stage for our home to become a classroom. I set aside space for teaching, bought school supplies, and started arranging the schedule so that I could have time set aside solely for teaching.

Even though my oldest was only three, I started immediately with formalized teaching time. This made the transition easier for when he was older because he was used to the routine of learning time, and was also used to working at his desk, even if it just meant coloring for five minutes.

I also declared my intention to homeschool to my extended family members, and to some of my friends. I did this because I knew that some of them would have a hard time with the idea, and I knew that others would completely support it. My friends and family who did support me made it easier to deal with those who didn't, and it was easier to get the criticism and second-guessing out of the way before I became absorbed with curriculum and scheduling decisions. It also gave me the opportunity to make it clear from the time that my children were very very young that although I appreciated the concern and well-meaning comments from others, I was ultimately responsible for the choices made for my family, and I would do what I believed was best.

Step-By-Step Guide to Getting Started

1. Declare your intention to homeschool. This will allow you to find the support that you need, and also allow you to deal with your critics. Criticism will come eventually, so you might as well get it out of the way.
2. Create a learning environment in your home.
3. Make it a point to set aside time to learn, so your children can get used to the idea of you being their teacher. It will help make the transition that much easier.
4. Buy the necessary supplies.
5. I have found that my children get very excited when we start shopping for the school supplies. It helps them transition into the school year, and makes them look forward to learning at home. I intentionally buy things a few days or even weeks before we need them to help build the anticipation.

What to Do

- Be confident with your decision.
- Share your decision with others and ask them to support you.

- Let your kids be excited about the decision to homeschool.
- Start creating a learning environment as early as you can. This will make the transition easier.

What Not To Do

- Do not feel that you have to be perfect.
- Do not be afraid to tell unsupportive people to keep their comments to themselves.
- Do not minimize the importance of learning.
- Do not diminish homeschool or refer to traditional schools as "real" schools.

Chapter 3: Choosing Your Curriculum

A Look In On Choosing Your Curriculum

When I first began considering what curriculum I was going to use, I was overwhelmed. There are many options out there, ranging from free to very expensive. And of course, I wanted to buy everything. I wanted to have a full library, three or four textbooks for every subject, and I wanted more worksheets than anyone could ever use. As I researched more, and as I considered my bank account, I narrowed it down to what I felt was essential.

Choosing your curriculum is important, but it doesn't need to be a cause for panic. Simply decide what suits your lifestyle best. There are several full curriculum kits out there, complete with text books, workbooks, and teacher's guides for every subject. There are both religious and non-religious choices.

You can also create your own curriculum. This is what I have done. I have looked over the educational standards and I have purchased a book which details what a classical education should include for every grade. I use that book as a launching point, and then supplement as needed. I use math workbooks, but I also create my own worksheets. I use science textbooks, but also check books out from the library.

I make sure that I cover all of the basic subjects with my children, but then I also enhance that based on what they are interested in at the time. For example, my oldest son was fascinated with snakes. So we spent an extra amount of time learning about snakes. My second son is all about black widows. So, unfortunately for me, we spent a lot of time researching black widows. My daughter wants to turn every lesson into a song and dance routine, and so we have created songs about math, words, history lessons, and art lessons.

My children learn a variety of things in a variety of ways, and no one curriculum could suit the diverse needs of my family. Therefore, I made my own.

Step-By-Step Guide to Choosing Your Curriculum

1. Consider what type of curriculum you are looking for.

    Do you want a religious curriculum? Do you want to use the same curriculum as the public schools? (If so, check with a charter school, or speak directly with your local Board of Education.) Do you feel comfortable creating your own curriculum?

2. Review the curriculum before you purchase.

This is a rule that I learned the hard way. I looked at a book online and thought it seemed perfect, but when I actually got it in my hands, it was way too simple. My son cruised through it in three weeks.

3. Choose a curriculum that will meet the needs of your family.

   This is one of the most fun aspects of homeschooling. You get to choose specifically for your children. Find areas that are of great interest to them and build around that.

4. Make sure that whichever curriculum you choose meets educational standards.

   Remember that your goal is to give your child a well-rounded and solid education. Do not forget about the basics.

What to Do

- Choose a curriculum which suits the needs of your family.
- Choose a curriculum that covers all of the basic subjects.
- Ask for help if you need it.

What Not To Do

- Do not feel that you need to purchase every curriculum option that is available.
- Do not think that you are stuck with whatever curriculum you choose. If you don't like it, you can change.
- Do not be afraid to mix and match from different sources.
- Do not hesitate to enhance the curriculum with other research and real life experience.

Chapter 4: Schedules

A Look In On Schedules

As I mentioned earlier in the guide, my husband and I are actively involved in youth work. This involvement means that we will go on trips to camps for weeks at time, attend weekend retreats, spend afterschool hours at sporting events and performances, and also that at any given time there are a number of teenagers in my home.

Our lifestyle has greatly enhanced my children's education. For example, we went to a youth camp a few weeks ago. At the camp, there was a large pond that had a huge number of tadpoles in various stages of metamorphosis. What better way was there for them to learn about the life cycle of a frog? Sure, they could read about it in a book, but they will never forget the sight of tadpoles with legs or frogs with tails.

Anyway, this section is about schedules. Our schedule changes a lot due to our travel, but here is a glimpse of a normal, non-traveling day at home:

8:00 – 8:30 - Breakfast and Morning Chores

8:30 – 8:45 – Get Into School Mode (Children gather books and supplies, I grab another cup of coffee and get into teacher mode)

8:45 – 9:00 - Journal Time

9:00 – 9:45 – Language Arts

9:45 – 10:15 – Science

10:15 – 10:30 – Break

10:30 – 11:15 – Math

11:15 – 11:45 – History

11:45 – 12:15 – Art/Music

12:15 – 1:15 – Lunch and Break

1:15 – 1:45 – Silent Reading Time

1:45 – 2:15   - PE

2:15 - 3:15 – Educational Television Shows

    I have found this schedule to work very well for my children. Although you may find it surprising to see television on the schedule, there are some excellent educational television shows for children. The other day my son said, "I have a hypothesis." He learned that from one of his favorite shows. PBS is my channel of choice.

    You will also notice that I have included a few minutes for me to get into teacher mode. This is a good time for me to put aside the pressures of household duties and focus on just being a teacher for my children. When I first started homeschooling, I would run around like crazy, trying to do laundry, wash dishes, and pay bills all while answering questions about math or history. This made me feel very stressed and frazzled, and that made the environment very tense, which affected my children. Now, I approach the school time like I have actually left the house and entered a classroom. The laundry and dishes can wait.

My children love having a schedule. They like to know what is coming up, and what to expect. They even ask for a schedule during the summer, and if I don't provide one, they create their own. There are some days, though, when I make a point to rip up the schedule and spend the day at the park or the pool. My children love these days, too.

Step-By-Step Guide to Schedules

- Create a schedule that will work for your family.

Do your kids work best early in the morning? Are you better in the afternoon? Do you have younger children who have a specific sleeping schedule? Tailor the school schedule around the needs of your family.

- Write the schedule down so everyone can see it.

Having the schedule written down serves several purposes. First, it provides accountability for you to stick to it. It can be easy to put things off and not devote as much time as you should to school if there is not a schedule posted. Second, it helps keep the day organized. The day will go much more smoothly if there is a schedule to follow. Third, it helps your children learn to tell time. As they begin to correlate the time on the schedule with the clock and the activity, they will learn about time.

- Adjust the schedule as needed.

Give the schedule two weeks to see if it works for your family. If by that time it isn't working, make adjustments as needed. Know that it isn't set in stone.

What to Do

- Create a schedule around the needs of your family.
- Allow for ample time to finish schoolwork.
- Schedule in time for regular breaks. Your children need, them and you do too.
- Post the schedule for everyone to see.

What Not To Do

- Do not be afraid to change the schedule if needed.
- Do not allow the schedule to interfere with natural learning opportunities. If your children are actively watching a spider spin its web, use it as a teaching time. Don't rush them inside to begin the next activity.
- Do not let the schedule cause undue stress. The schedule is supposed to be a help to the process, not a hindrance.

- Don't forget to consider other activities when making the schedule.

Chapter 5: Assessment

A Look In On Assessment

Assessment can be a difficult area for homeschoolers. Some states require standardized testing (more on that in the legal section), but others do not. My children are not required to sit for the standardized tests, but I do feel that it is important to assess where they are and to determine if the homeschooling is effective.

My second oldest thrives under the pressure of a test. He is a competitive child and looks to beat the clock and his score. I have found it easier to assess where he is at. I give him regular tests to see how he is performing, and adjust from there. My oldest, however, does not do well with tests. He is a perfectionist and almost freezes up if he is given a traditional test. For him, I adjust how I assess him. I have him complete the tests to make sure that he knows the material, but I do not time him, and I do not inform him it is a test. I can still see how he is doing, but he does not get stressed out.

Another way that I assess to see how my children are doing is by checking out the state standards. The state educational websites give lists of the educational standards, and you can check to see if your children are on track.

Something to remember with assessment, though, is that by choosing to homeschool, you have given yourself the freedom to work with your child's strengths and weaknesses. For example, my oldest is well above grade level in mathematics and reading, but his writing abilities are below grade level. He has struggled with his fine motor skills since he was an infant, and that is apparent in his writing difficulties. He knows what he wants to say, but actually forming the letters on paper is not easy for him. I address this by having him work on writing about things that he is excited about, but I also don't force the issue. I don't make a big deal about it to him, but I am acutely aware that it is an area in which he needs to improve, so I schedule activities accordingly.

I want my children to understand that it is important to regularly evaluate how they are doing and to learn from and correct mistakes, but I also do not want them to become obsessed with letter grades and scores. I do not want their identity to be wrapped up with how they perform in school. Because I am their teacher, I can help make sure this happens.

This area of assessment is one that I have learned gradually. I was a straight-A student in high school. I graduated as the valedictorian, did very well on achievement tests, and went to college on a full educational scholarship. Unfortunately, I also allowed my self-worth to become wrapped up in my school performance, and I struggled. I worked through that while in college, but when I began homeschooling, I knew of no other way to assess outside of letter grades. I had to check myself and my tendencies and realize that I was starting to slip back into old habits. This led me to look at other ways to determine if my children were learning.

Step-By-Step Guide to Assessment

1. Determine the assessment method that will work best with your child.

   Does your child do well with tests? Would an oral assessment work better than a written one? Are you required to administer standardized tests?

2. Do regular assessments to make sure your child is learning.

   They do not need to be elaborate exams. Sometimes I will just ask my kids to tell their dad what they learned at school that day. That in itself is an assessment tool.

3. Keep assessment in perspective.

   Do not forget that your child is more than just a grade or a test score. You know if your child is learning. You know his strengths and weaknesses. It is important to assess your child's learning, but no test can capture everything.

What to Do

- Assess your child according to his or her learning style.
- Pay attention to areas in which your child needs extra work.

- Recognize the areas in which your child is excelling.
- Relax about assessments. Assessment gives you something to work from, but in no way gives a complete picture of your child's educational experience.

What Not To Do

- Do not compare your children to other children. Each child learns in a different way and at a different pace. Do not measure the success of your children based on other children.
- Do not worry about assessment results. Work on the weaknesses and build on the strengths.
- Do not let your children feel that they are defined by their assessment scores. Again, your child is more than a grade.
- Do not compare your children to other children. I know I already mentioned this, but it cannot be said enough. It can be very harmful for a child to feel that they are being compared to other children. Recognize what is unique about each child, and do not compare.

Chapter 6: Socializing

A Look In On Socializing

Socializing of children is probably one of the most talked about issues when it comes to homeschooling children. I know that when I first made the decision to homeschool, socializing was the issue brought the most concern for people. I heard a range of comments, from the helpful ("How do you intend on helping your children in their social development, especially with their peers?") to the annoying, ("Your kids are going to turn into weird, homeschool freaks.") I learned to separate the good from the bad, and managed to hold my tongue with the merely annoying.

This issue is not near as difficult as some make it seem. There are a wide range of opportunities for children to be able to interact with their peers. Many areas have homeschooling communities in which all of the families get together once or twice a week. This allows the children to have normal social interaction, and also allows the families to support and encourage each other.

I will tell you how I have handled the whole social issue with my children. I am not a part of a homeschooling community. As I have mentioned, we travel a lot and have a lot of other commitments within the community, so I have chosen not to become a part of the homeschool network. This is not to say that my children do not interact with their peers. We are actively involved in a local church which has a large children's program, and my sons play soccer and baseball, and my daughter will be enrolling in dance classes. We frequent the neighborhood parks and pools, and I make it a point to bring my children to places where other children congregate. My children have no trouble making friends and fitting in.

About a year ago I noticed that the majority of influences on my children were teenagers, and I did something about that. Although the kids we've been surrounded by have been great kids, my six year old started acting like he thought he was sixteen. I countered this by cutting back on the time spent with teens and increasing the time spent with other younger children.

As a parent, I realize that it is my duty to help my children become well-rounded people. I am responsible for their development, and I make an active effort to give them opportunities in which to thrive. I love the fact that my children are able to converse easily with people of all ages, from children through older adults. They have learned to communicate.

My children may be a bit naïve, and a bit less aware of some of the things their peers are well-versed in, but that's all right with me. They will grow up fast enough as it is. They don't need to rush it just to fit in with the neighbors.

As long as you are aware of the situation and make an effort to allow your children to have regular interaction with their peers, they will be fine.

Oh, and as far as the comment that my children would become "homeschool freaks" – I simply responded that my husband and I are both considered odd and somewhat freakish, and we both went to public school. That ended the discussion!

Step-By-Step Guide to Socializing

1. Make it a priority to allow your children to interact with their peers.

    Children need time to be around other children. They need to learn to interact with their peers, and they need time to develop social skills. It is possible to do this even while homeschooling. You just need to remember that it's important.

2. Find ways for your child to socialize.

    Just like adults, children find it easier to build friendships when they have something in common with other children. If your child is into sports, sign her up for a sports team. If your child is into music, have him join a youth band or orchestra. Also, consider homeschooling communities.

3. Go where there are children.

    If you see kids at the park, stop and let your kids play. It's that simple.

4. Don't force the issue.

   If your child is not overly social and only has a few friends, that's okay. Don't force your child to be something he's not. My oldest son is very reserved, and he prefers to play with one or two children at a time. He is drawn to the more intellectual children, and he loves sitting and talking with his closest friends. My second son, however, is a social butterfly. He is always at the heart of a large group of children and loves meeting new people. They are both social in their own way.

What to Do

- Provide opportunities for your children to socialize with other children.
- Allow your children to invite their friends to come and play.
- Seek out ways for your children to meet new friends.

What Not To Do

- Do not worry that your children will not be normal. Is anyone ever completely normal?
- Do not think that just because your child only has a few friends, he or she is unhappy. Some children only want a few friends.

- Do not feel that just because you homeschool you have to be alone. There are several resources available for you for company.

Chapter 7: Legal Issues

A Look In On Legal Issues

To some people, the legal issue of homeschooling may be the most confusing part of the whole thing. It may even seem scary. In reality, though, it's not that difficult.

A simple internet search will direct you to websites which clearly outline the specific homeschool guidelines for your state. All you need to do is read those guidelines and follow them. For some states, it's as simple as choosing to homeschool your child and if anyone asks about it, you just need to state that you are homeschooling. Other states require forms to be submitted, while others require that you meet with a licensed teacher to have your curriculum approved.

For most states there are exceptions for religious reasons, as well as options to register with private schools. Research the laws for your particular state, and then make your decision accordingly.

I have had no problem with the legality of homeschooling my children. I simply fill out a form saying that I will be homeschooling my children, and I'm free to do as I see best for my family.

The first year that I officially homeschooled, I enrolled with an online private school. I sent regular reports to them about my son's progress, sent in attendance reports, and sent in samples of his work. They in turn sent me a letter at the end of the year verifying that he was, indeed, a student during that year. I spent that summer researching more about the options in my state, and I learned that I could sign up to be my own private school. It cost nothing, and only took a bit of paperwork. I did that, and it was a lot easier, and less expensive.

This is one area in which a homeschooling community can be a huge asset. Contact a group in your area and ask them for advice. You can see what other homeschooling families are doing, and make the best choice for you.

Step-By-Step Guide to Legal Issues

1. Research the legal requirements for homeschoolers for your state.
2. Take whatever steps are necessary to homeschool your child.
3. Relax. As long as you are abiding by the law, you are fine.

What to Do

- Make sure that you are informed. Do the research that you need to do.
- Do whatever is necessary to abide by the law.
- Realize that you have the right to homeschool. Sometimes you may have to fill out paperwork or have your child take exams to exercise this right, but the right is yours.

What Not To Do

- Do not ignore the requirements set forth by your state. You may not agree with the requirements, but it's always best to adhere to the law.
- Do not make the legal issue bigger than it needs to be. It may be a hassle at times to fill out paperwork or meet with licensed teachers, but it's a hassle you chose when you chose to homeschool.
- Do not be afraid to ask for help. There are legal defense funds and associations dedicated to helping homeschoolers have the right to continue homeschooling. If anyone challenges your right, get help.

Conclusion

A Look In On Homeschooling

I truly enjoy homeschooling my children. I love the freedom that I have to choose what my children learn, and I love seeing their faces light up when they understand a new concept. My fridge is full of papers they have completed, and I cherish the sound of my son reading aloud to me. My oldest son teaches the second oldest. He teaches his little sister. And she is teaching the baby. Even when the school year ends, the learning and teaching never does.

Homeschooling has been the best choice for my family, and one that I plan on continuing to do as long as it provides the best education for my kids. Both my husband and I have experience in tutoring all subjects up through high school, and we feel confident in our abilities. We know that more and more colleges are recognizing homeschooling as a viable educational choice, and that a large number of students admitted to top schools have come from homeschools.

To me, the very best part of homeschooling is the freedom that it provides. A few months ago we took a cross country trip with our children. They were able to learn about geography and cultures and history in a way that no book could ever teach them. They didn't write a report, and they didn't fill out a worksheet, but they learned. And they remember. This was something that we wouldn't have been able to do had they been enrolled in a traditional school.

Not all families are like mine. Not all children would thrive in the homeschool environment. But mine do, and my family is better for it.

Top 9 Things to Remember

1. **The decision to homeschool is one that you need to make based on what is best for your family.**

    I have made several decisions that many people would not have made for themselves, but, surprisingly, my decision to homeschool has been the one that has caused the most conflict. People in my circle feel very passionately about the subject. I just remind myself that I need to do what is best for my family. When other people talk to me about homeschooling, I always encourage them to do the same. And while most people are encouraged and continue with their decision to homeschool, some have realized that they were only deciding to homeschool because their friends did. Again, choose what is best for your own family.

2. **Do not compare you children to other children.**

    I told you this can't be said enough! Each child is unique, with specific gifts and abilities, and needs to be treated as such. Do not make educational decisions for your child based on what other children are doing. Yes, your child needs to learn to read. But your child needs to learn to read because it's a skill that will help him for the rest of his life, not because your friend's son is five years old and reading full length novels. Appreciate what is unique about each child.

3. **Homeschooling is not for everyone.**

    If you have considered homeschooling and have decided that it is not best for your family, there's nothing wrong with that! I love homeschooling. It is the best situation for my family. Nevertheless, I realize that not everyone has the same schedule that I do, not everyone has the passion for homeschooling that I do, and not everyone has the freedom that I do. This world would be an incredibly boring place if everyone had to make the same choices!

4. **Work with the strengths and weaknesses of your children.**

    The beauty of homeschooling is that you can work to the strengths of your children. You can find what interests and excites them. You can see what is working and what isn't, and you can tailor things accordingly. You have so much freedom! Take advantage of it.

5. **It is important for you to set the tone that education matters.**

This is something that I am extremely passionate about, and not just when it comes to homeschooling. Parents need to set the tone that education is important. Whether it is done at home or in a traditional school setting, your children need to learn, from you, that it is essential that they learn.

I have seen far too many parents who treat their children's education like it is less important than other endeavors. It is no wonder to me that those children end up struggling in school, having a bad attitude, and often times get in trouble at school. If a child has not been shown that school is valuable, why should we expect him to desire to excel?

The best thing that you can do for your children is develop in them a love for learning. Let them see you reading and learning. Ask them about what they have learned. Praise them for learning new things, and let them know that excelling in school is just as important as excelling in sports, or music, or any other area.

6. Set a schedule that works with your family.

This is important to remember because you want the homeschool experience to be positive for everyone. Don't set a schedule that will leave you feeling stressed and anxious. Don't set a schedule which conflicts with sleeping patterns or other commitments.

Also, remember to allow for flexibility in your schedule. Some of the best learning times with my children have come when the schedule has gone out the window, and we have spent an entire morning reading a novel or watching bugs or planting a garden.

7. **Realize that you can always change your mind.**

    Do not feel that you are trapped into homeschooling. If it just isn't working for your family, or if your children are not thriving, then you can go back to traditional school, or even modified homeschooling. Several school districts have charter schools which allow for most of the learning to be done at home, but also offer structured classroom times. Some private schools offer part-time homeschooling options, where students can attend the classroom for half of the day, and complete the rest of the lessons at home. Research all of your options, and choose the one that is best for your family.

8. **Make it a point to give your children opportunities to socialize with their peers.**

    The very nature of homeschooling means that your children will have less interaction with their peers than they would in a traditional school setting. If children are not given the opportunity to interact with their peers, this can cause delays in their social development.

This is an issue that can easily be solved by action on your part. Seek out opportunities for your children to interact with their peers. There are church activities, camps, sports teams, lessons, or even days at the park that can give your children time with kids their own ages.

I have four children, and they spend a lot of time playing together. Whenever they get the opportunity, though, they find kids their own age to play with. It always has a good effect on them, and I have found that after spending time with other children, they have more patience for their siblings.

9. Homeschooling provides a lot of freedom, but it also requires a lot of work.

I guess this is not always true, but it should be. If you are homeschooling for the right reason – which is to make sure your child is learning in the best environment for his particular needs, and in a way that enhances your family – then you will be committed to providing the best education possible.

This means taking the time to create lesson plans, read articles and books, and search for opportunities to help your children learn.

It is true that there are a lot of educational television shows available for children. I regularly let my children watch these shows. But the television is not their teacher. I am. And I take my responsibility seriously.

To go back to the quote from Aristotle, homeschooling provides the amazing opportunity to be the person who not only gave your child life, but also the art of living well.

This guide was by no means intended to be the be-all and end-all on the subject of homeschooling. There are so many things to learn, and so many things to discover.

The best thing to do once you have decided to homeschool is to dive in with your children, and see how they learn. Some children will learn by reading, others by seeing, and others by doing. Take the time to see what is unique about your child's learning style. It can be a very fun time, and can also provide invaluable insight.

Cherish this time with your children. They will learn and grow so fast, and before you know it they will be entering college. Make the homeschooling time a fun time. Don't view it as a chore, or as something you have to get over with. View it as a time to learn and grow alongside your child. You'll be glad you did.

About the Expert

Jane Rodda holds a Bachelor's Degree in Liberal Studies with a concentration in Psychology from Point Loma Nazarene University in San Diego, California. She is a homeschooling mother of four who lives in Nashville, Tennessee. Having worked as a classroom teacher before having children, she felt confident in her abilities to homeschool, and made the decision when her oldest was three years old. She currently has children in Kindergarten, First Grade, and Fourth Grade.

In addition to homeschooling her own children, Jane has also worked as a private tutor. As a tutor, she has had the opportunity to work with students from a wide range of educational backgrounds, from homeschoolers, to public and private school students, to college students. She has witnessed the effects of each schooling option, and tries to incorporate the positive aspects of each she has seen while avoiding the negative.

Jane wrote How to Homeschool Your Children because she desires to help others learn from her experience. She is passionate about learning and educating, and wants to help guide others as they begin their homeschooling journey.

Jane feels that her life and the lives of her children have been enriched by their homeschooling experience, and she seeks to encourage other parents to homeschool with confidence.

Recommended Resources

- HowExpert.com – Quick 'How To' Guides on All Topics from A to Z by Everyday Experts.
- HowExpert.com/free – Free HowExpert Email Newsletter.
- HowExpert.com/books – HowExpert Books
- HowExpert.com/courses – HowExpert Courses
- HowExpert.com/clothing – HowExpert Clothing
- HowExpert.com/membership – HowExpert Membership Site
- HowExpert.com/affiliates – HowExpert Affiliate Program
- HowExpert.com/writers – Write About Your #1 Passion/Knowledge/Expertise & Become a HowExpert Author.
- HowExpert.com/resources – Additional HowExpert Recommended Resources
- YouTube.com/HowExpert – Subscribe to HowExpert YouTube.
- Instagram.com/HowExpert – Follow HowExpert on Instagram.
- Facebook.com/HowExpert – Follow HowExpert on Facebook.

Printed in Great Britain
by Amazon

58115062R00031